Reading in two parts

Work with a partner.
Each of you taking a different part, read and sing this melody using solfa:

Each singer sings two phrases
Each phrase is two bars long.

Change parts and sing the melody again.

Which two phrases are the same ?

Working in two parts

These phrases are short in both upper and lower parts.
But they are different from each other.

The phrases in the upper part
are one bar long.
But the phrases in the
lower part are two bars long.

As a partner sings the
lower part, invent new 1-bar
phrases for the upper part.

Reading and performing

Here is more music in two parts.
The first piece is in rhythm-solfa and uses the doh hexachord.

With a partner, read and sing the upper part several times.
Repeat it, until you know it well. Then do the same with the lower part.
When you are confident, sing the music in two parts.

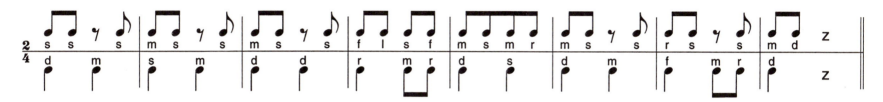

Sing this many times, until you know both parts well and can sing them from memory.

Play the music from memory on two keyboard instruments:
- first, play with doh = F
- then, play with doh = G.

The parts in
this piece use
the doh
pentachord.

After singing it, talk with your partner about the phrases.
Are they the same? Are they different?

Sharing parts

With a partner, read and practise both parts.

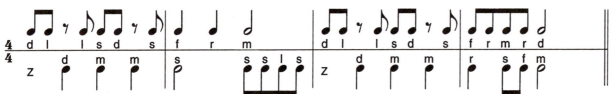

When you are ready, sing the piece in two parts.
Change parts and repeat.

Work with a partner again, practising both parts.

Then sing in two parts.
Change parts and repeat.
Perform the piece again – this time, humming both parts.

Music for different purposes

You have thought about how music is used in everyday life.
It can express the way we feel – and it can change the way we feel.

Sing this piece with a partner.
Play this piece on a keyboard instrument from memory (doh = C).

Work in a group of three (each with a different
type of percussion instrument).

Singing and/or playing the melody, and improvising
with the percussion, make a piece of music which is
  (i)   solemn (or even sad)
 (ii)   lively (or happy)
(iii)   frightening.

Think about your tempo, timbre (tone colour of
the instruments) and special effects,
e.g. sudden loud notes in a quiet performance.

Music can be used for many purposes. Add words to make this piece a television advert.

Traditional hymns

Here is a hymn to sing at the end of the school day.

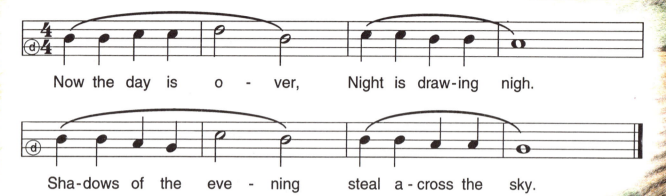

Now the day is o - ver, Night is draw-ing nigh.

Sha-dows of the eve - ning steal a - cross the sky.

Does it use a tetrachord, pentachord or hexachord?
How many pulses do you feel to a whole note?

Learn this melody to solfa names.
Sing it from memory.
Then play it from memory (doh = C):
 (i) on a pitched percussion instrument;
(ii) on an electronic keyboard.

Compare the way whole notes sound on each instrument.
The sound of a whole note needs to be held for its full length.
The voice does this well.

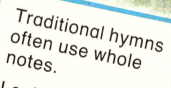

Traditional hymns often use whole notes.

Look in a church hymn book to see how often whole notes are used.

A new day

Here are words for the first verse of a hymn.

New day is dawning,
Sleep and slumber done,
Now comes the morning
Wakened by the sun.

Speak them in rhythm; the first line could be like this:

$\frac{4}{4}$ ♩ ♩ ♩ | ♩ ♩ |

New day is dawn - ing,

Perhaps some of the composed hymns could be sung in the school assembly.

Write your rhythm for the whole hymn on Writing Sheet 2 (upper).

Try to include whole notes, half notes and quarter notes.

Use the doh pentachord to make a melody in rhythm-solfa.

Then write your hymn tune in staff notation on Writing Sheet 2 (lower).

Write more verses for your hymn.

Canons

Sing this melody with your partner, using solfa names.
When you are confident, sing it together in canon, as written.

You can see clearly how the lower part follows the upper part.

Here is a canon which is different.
Sing the upper part of the canon; ask your partner to sing the lower part.

At first, it might not sound like a canon.
The lower part has the same shape, but it is at a different pitch.
But this is a canon – the lower part is simply one note higher all the way through the piece.

Longer canons

With canons, the second part always follows later.

This is a longer canon.
Learn it with a partner and then perform it in canon.

The first part has an extra bar near the end; so the two parts finish together.

Goblins

This song uses the new note, low lah (l₁).
Sing it with your partner.
It is called 'The Goblin Song'.

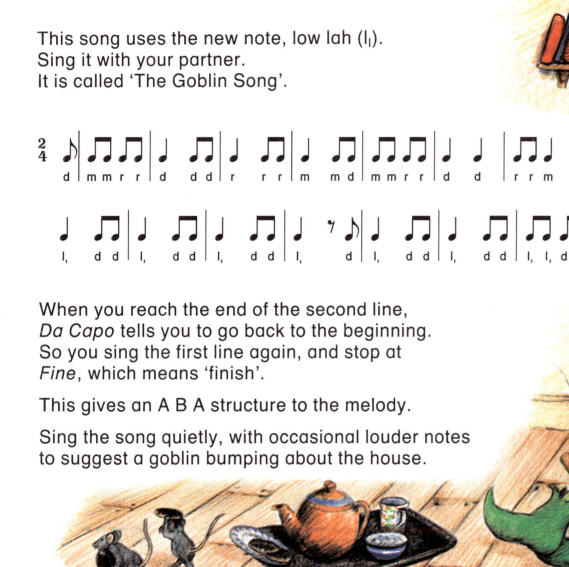

When you reach the end of the second line,
Da Capo tells you to go back to the beginning.
So you sing the first line again, and stop at
Fine, which means 'finish'.

This gives an A B A structure to the melody.

Sing the song quietly, with occasional louder notes
to suggest a goblin bumping about the house.

The pick-up note

With a partner, look closely at this rhythm from the beginning of
'The Goblin Song'.
Sing the words shown while tapping a pulse.
You will feel that the strong beat is on '**go**-blin', not on the first word 'A'.

In written music, the note value of the pick-up note at the beginning counts as part of the total value of the final bar at the end.

So '**go**-blin' is placed on the first beat of the bar.
'A' is given a separate eighth note before the first bar line;
this is known as a **pick-up note** or **anacrusis**.

Here is the melody of 'Oh, who will shoe?'. It begins with a quarter note 'pick-up'.
Sing the song, marking the first beat of each bar with a tap.

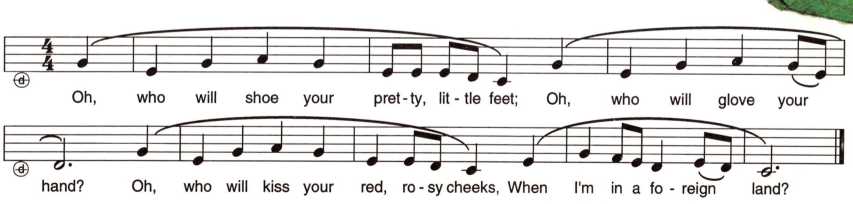

Play 'Oh, who will shoe?' from memory on a keyboard instrument (doh = C or G).

Two parts again

Here is 'The Goblin Song' with its words.
Tap the pulse as you sing it to solfa with a partner.
Then sing it to the words.

Now, one partner sings phrases 1 and 2, and the other sings phrases 3 and 4.
Both sing the repeat from *Da Capo* to *Fine*.

A go-blin lives in our house, in our house, in our house, A go-blin lives in our house all the year round. He bumps and he jumps and he thumps and he stumps, He knocks and he rocks and he rat-tles at the locks.

Look for low lah in this two-part piece.

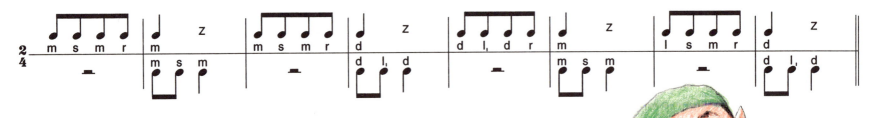

With a partner, learn to sing it from memory.
Then play it from memory as a duet, each using a separate melodic instrument (doh = F).

Low lah (l₁) in staff notation and rhythm-solfa   p.32

Magic and spells

Here are the rhythm and words of a different goblin song.

Go - blin you have   mag - ic pow'rs,   Ma - king spells for   hours and hours:

Eye of bat and   root of tree;   Will you make a   spell for me?

Compose a melody in rhythm-solfa:

- use this rhythm
- use d and r and l₁ only
- use Writing Sheet 2 (upper).

Then write your melody in staff notation:

- use Writing Sheet 2 (lower);
- add the words to your finished melody;
- ask others in the class to read and
  sing your melody, using a voice
  that suggests magic and mystery.

The cruel giant

Music can help to tell a story.

> There once lived an ugly giant in a large castle. He was very greedy and very selfish and never had kind thoughts for others. Over the years he became cruel and ruthless! He would capture people from the village and make them work as slaves in his cold, dark castle.

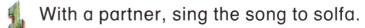

1   With a partner, sing the song to solfa.

2   Look at the way the song is built:
Tone-set   s-f-m-r-d-l,
Rhythm-set ♩ ♩
Phrases   A B C D B

3   Sing verses 1 and 2 with a 'cruel' (hard, unpleasant) voice.

4   How could you use percussion to make the song more frightening?

Song of the Cruel Giant

(Verse 3 has words which the slaves sing.)

MUSIC IN OUR LIVES

1 In my cas - tle here I stand, I have slaves to
2 All are pleased to work for me, I am ve - ry
3 Hard the work and long the hours, Sub - ject to our

work my land; I have slaves to clean and sweep;
kind, you see. Work - ing twen - ty hours each day,
mas - ter's pow'rs. To our tasks our backs we bend,

I have slaves who ne - ver sleep. In my cas - tle here I stand.
With no food and with no pay. All are pleased to work for me.
Will our sad - ness ne - ver end? Hard the work and long the hours.

Sea creatures

Fishes have a streamlined shape, so they glide smoothly through water.
This song is about the movement of sea creatures underwater.
Sing the song with a partner, first to solfa, then with the words.

Fish are glid-ing, ___ Gleam-ing, glid-ing, ___ Un-der wa-ter, ___ Un-der wa-ter, ___ Shells are

curl-ing, ___ Furl-ing, curl-ing, ___ Un-der wa-ter, ___ Un-der wa-ter, ___ There are

crea-tures ___ strange and free ___ In the sea, ___ In the sea. ___

Some notes in this song have been made longer
by 'tying' them to other notes of the same pitch.
This produces an effect rather like the gentle push and
glide of a fish as it moves forward through the water.

Copy this rhythm on to paper; add 'ties' and solfa names
to produce a new melody of similar effect.

Then add your own words
about swimming fish.

Tied notes 📖 p.35

'Spooky' and 'Not-so-spooky'

Melodies are not always based on doh.

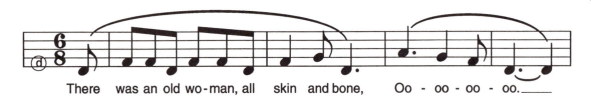

There was an old wo-man, all skin and bone, Oo - oo - oo - oo.____

This low lah melody sounds quite 'spooky' – or even sad.

But a low lah melody can also be cheerful:

Cap-tain, go side - track your train, Cap-tain, go side - track your train,

Num-ber one in line, com-ing in on time, Cap-tain, go side - track your train.

Sing both melodies and learn them by heart.
Play both melodies, from memory, on a keyboard instrument (lah = A).

Melodies based on l₁ p.38

Make sure you are creating the right 'mood' by the way you perform.

Haunted house

Compose a slow-moving melody to sing about a derelict house on a dark night.

Make a recording of your song for the class to listen to with eyes closed.

Use:
- the time signature $\frac{2}{4}$
- the tone-set   m-r-d-l₁
- the rhythm-set ♫ ♩ ♩ z
- the structure   A A B C.

Write your melody in staff notation on Writing Sheet 1.

Add suitable words.

Working with your partner, prepare this two-part piece for performance:
 (i) as slow, eerie music for a dark, misty night;
 (ii) as a piece hummed or whistled by a cheerful delivery boy/girl.

Lullaby

Ho, ho,— wa-ta-nay, Ho, ho,— wa-ta-nay, Ho, ho,— wa-ta-nay, Ki yo-ke na, Ki yo-ke na.

This lullaby is sung by the Iroquois people of North America.

It is a melody which includes the new note **low soh (s₁)**
– one note lower than low lah (l₁).
Sing it with a partner.

Below is a rhythm for a gentle lullaby.

Use this rhythm and these words to make your own North American Indian lullaby.

- Use m-r-d-l₁-s₁.
- Make it a lah-based melody, starting and ending with low lah (l₁).
- Compose three bars to each phrase.

Now go to sleep, lit-tle ba - by, Now go to sleep, lit-tle one.

Sing your lullaby to your partner.
(If your partner goes to sleep, it is a good lullaby!)

Pentatone patterns

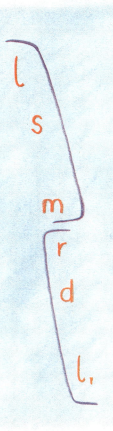

Work with a partner.

Improvise a short phrase (using upper section).

For example: $\frac{4}{4}$ ♩ ♫♩ ♩ ‖

                  s   l   l   s   m

The partner repeats the phrase (using lower section).

For example: $\frac{4}{4}$ ♩ ♫♩ ♩ ‖

                  d   r   r   d   l,

Improvise, and repeat, other phrases in this way.

Then improvise in the lower section, making repeats from the upper section.

By improvising and repeating, compose an 8-bar melody to this pattern:

Write it in rhythm-solfa (Writing Sheet 2).

New patterns with the pentatone

This pentatone includes **s₁**.
Notice that **r** belongs to both sections – upper and lower.

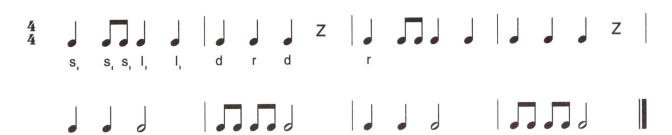

Work with a partner.
Complete this melody by composing and repeating phrases as before:

Then write the complete melody in staff notation (Writing Sheet 1).
Choose a position for ⓓ so that all notes fit on the staff.

Upstairs and downstairs

Sing these phrases, with a partner.

d   r   m   s   l   s   m   s, l, d   r   m   r   d

The first phrase is from the upper section.
The second phrase repeats, from the lower section;
it moves in the same direction, by starting on s_l.

Here is another version:

d   r   m   s   l   s   m   m   r   d   l,   s,   l,   d

The first phrase is from the upper section, as before.
The second phrase repeats from the lower section, as before;
but this time, moving in the opposite direction (rather like a mirror).

Here is a new first phrase:

d   d   r   r   m s l s m

With a partner, sing a second phrase, moving in the same
direction, starting on s_l.
Then sing a second phrase, moving in the opposite
direction, starting on **m**.

Work with this starting phrase in the same way:

d   d   r   r   m   s m

Repetition and sequence

Jo and Louise have been asked to add to this phrase.

Jo has used the same
phrase again.

Louise has used the same phrase again,
but she has placed it one note lower.

A repeated phrase at
the same pitch is
REPETITION.

A repeated phrase at a different
pitch (higher or lower) is
SEQUENCE.

Sing this melody with a partner.
How much repetition and how much sequence can you find?

Preparing for a class concert

Start with this opening to compose an 8-bar (A B) melody.
Work with a partner.
Use the doh hexachord, with much repetition and sequence.

... etc.

Listen for repetition and sequence.

Now make changes to your melody:

keep some of the repetition;
keep some of the sequence.

Think about the shape of your melody line.
Think about the balance of your phrase.

Then write out the finished melody in staff notation.

Have a concert in class.

Decide how you would like to have it performed:

- solo voice? (should it have words?)
- small choir? (using members of the class?)
- solo instrument? (played from memory, doh = G or C)

Working with others in the class, make arrangements
to rehearse and perform your melody.

Summers past and to come

You have already used the time signatures $\frac{2}{4}$, $\frac{6}{8}$ and $\frac{4}{4}$.
This song has a simple time metre of 3 beats. So it has a time signature of $\frac{3}{4}$.

Sum - mer good - bye, Sum - mer good - bye, Ro - ses their pe - tals__shed,

Ap - ples are turn - ing__ red, Sum - mer good - bye, Sum - mer good - bye.

Sing the melody.
How many phrases does this melody have?
Label the phrases to show the structure.
Can you find repetition?
Can you find sequence?

Compose a melody in $\frac{3}{4}$ to the same phrase structure as 'Summer goodbye'.
Write it directly in staff notation (Writing Sheet 1).

Start your melody like this:

Now sum-mer-time has come,

The song is to be called
'Now summertime has come'.
Add suitable words to complete your melody.

The cheerful old woman

Here is another story:

> *There was once an old woman who lived in a cottage near the wood. She was always cheerful and always kind, even at the most difficult times. For example, when her washing blew down in the mud, she sang verse 1 of this song.*

The song tells us about her other misfortunes.

Form a group of six. Practise performing the song, with each person choosing a solo verse to sing. All sing 'Well, well, well' as a chorus. Then perform the song, with instrumentalists playing the accompaniment taught by the teacher. After rehearsals, each group performs in turn to the rest of the class.

	Well!	Well!	Well!	Some	black chim-ney smut-tings have
1	Well!	Well!	Well!	By	turn-ing so so-ur the
2	Well!	Well!	Well!	To	make from soft this-tle-down
3	Well!	Well!	Well!	Be-cause I fell o-ver u-
4	Well!	Well!	Well!	The	eggs are all bro-ken a-
5	Well!	Well!	Well!	My	cot-tage which now has burn'd

blown this way, So I need to wash it a-gain to-day. It
milk can be Some ve-ry good cheese for my grand-child's tea. It
I in-tend A beau-ti-ful pin cu-shion for my friend. It
pon the stair My blue patch-work quilt I shall now re-pair. It
bout my feet But warm scram-bled eggs are a spe-cial treat. It
to the ground Was sub-ject to draughts and to leaks, I've found. It

real-ly is luck-y, you see _____ That this should now hap-pen to

last time

me. _____ Well! Well! Well!

For a story: the cheerful old woman 📖 p.48 **25**

Five notes on a xylophone

Here is a doh pentachord, in staff notation:

ASCENDING

DESCENDING

Play the doh pentachord on a xylophone.

If your instrument has a wide range of notes, you will be able to play it in two different positions on the 'white' notes of the xylophone.

For example, on a xylophone with this range of notes:

When doh = C, the pentachord builds up to include these notes:

soh
fah
me
ray
doh

G
F
E
D
C

When doh = G, the pentachord builds up to include these notes:

D
C
B
A
G

soh
fah
me
ray
doh

Fixed pitch: the doh pentachord 📖 p.49

The G clef

This is the G clef.

It shows us where the note G is placed on the staff.

So, the G doh pentachord is written:

G A B C D

And therefore, the C doh pentachord is written:

C D E F G

Using a xylophone, play one of these pentachords to your partner (ascending or descending):

- the partner sings it to solfa;
- the partner sings it to letter names.

By joining the two pentachords, we produce a wide range of notes:

C D E F G A B C D

Reading with the G clef

The melodies on this page have a G-Clef.
With a partner, prepare Part A by using
these three methods of performance.

Try performing in
two parts, combining
different methods.

Method 1 Sing the melody to solfa names
(solfa given under first note).

Method 2 Sing the melody to letter names.

Method 3 Play the melody on a keyboard instrument,
according to the letter names.

Part A

me

Prepare Part B using Methods 1, 2 and 3.

Part B

soh

Rehearse both parts together, one partner taking Part A, the other taking Part B;
then perform in two parts, using each Method in turn.

Six notes on a xylophone

We already know about the doh hexachord.

$$\frac{3}{4}$$ ♩ ♩ ♩ | ♩ ♩ ♩ | ♩ ♩ ♩ | ♩ 𝅗𝅥 | 𝅗𝅥 ♩ ‖

d r m   f s l   s f m   r d

Using the xylophone, play the doh hexachord in two different positions:
 (i) starting on C;
(ii) starting on G.

The note arrangement on a xylophone will look like this:

Sing this melody, then play it on a xylophone or keyboard:

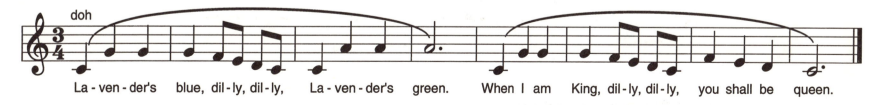

La - ven - der's blue, dil - ly, dil - ly, La - ven - der's green. When I am King, dil - ly, dil - ly, you shall be queen.

Then from memory, play it using the doh hexachord on G.

The fox and the grapes

Here is a melody for dancing.
This is a British folk dance tune, called 'The Fox and the Grapes'.

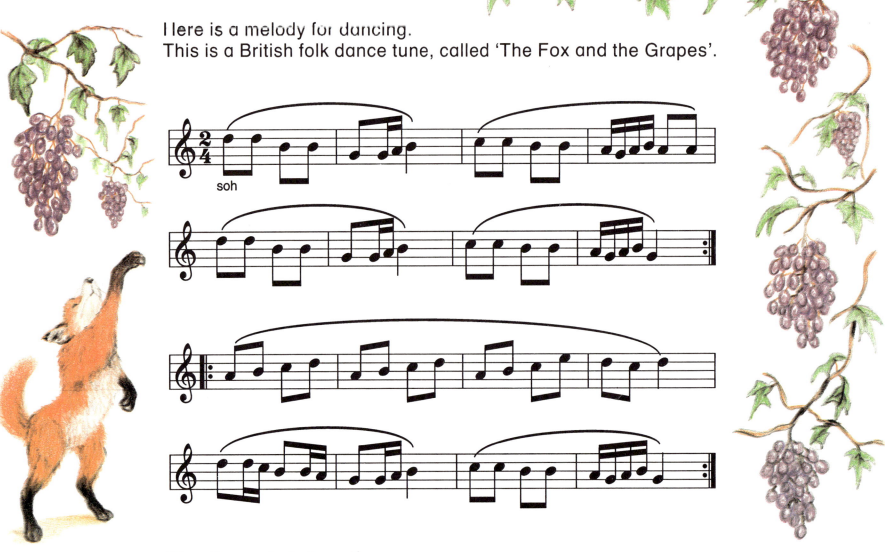

Sing the melody to solfa.
Play the melody on a keyboard or pitched percussion instrument.

Folk dance and the sixteenth note (1) p.54

Folk dancing

The Fox and the Grapes

This melody has 8 bars, which repeat (Section A).
Then it has 8 more bars, which repeat (Section B).

Make 'The Fox and the Grapes' longer.

Compose 8 extra bars, which repeat (Section C).
Use sixteenth notes.
Write in staff notation (doh = G).

Form a group of six:

- Perform the longer melody and invent a circle dance to fit the music.
- Practise your dance and make improvements.
- Perform your dance for others in the class.

Making up a folk dance

Here are some melodic ideas for making a folk dance.
Changing pitch is important, since too much repetition becomes tiresome.

Sing, then play on a keyboard or pitched percussion instrument, melody **A1**.

A1

doh

Sing, then play, melody **A2**. This is the same as melody **A1**, but at a higher pitch.

A2

doh

Melodies **B1** and **C1** are different. Sing them, play them and learn them by heart.

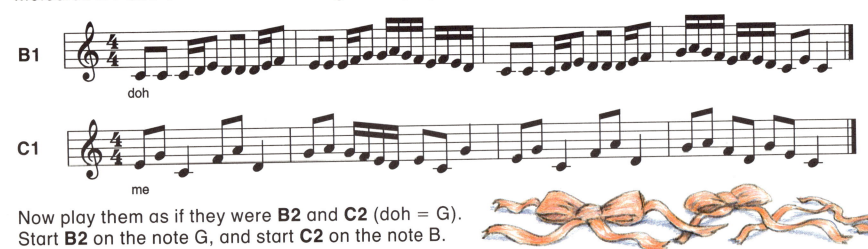

B1

doh

C1

me

Now play them as if they were **B2** and **C2** (doh = G).
Start **B2** on the note G, and start **C2** on the note B.

Starting a folk band

Several melodies are needed to accompany one dance.
Often, to keep the music interesting, a new melody will be played with a different doh.

Use the melodies on page 32 as music for a folk dance.

Make a pattern of melodies, for example:

A1	A1	A2	A1	B2	B2	A1	C2	C2	A1

Form a group of five or six people.

Perform this pattern with combinations of suitable instruments:

- Instruments of limited pitch might play only some sections.
- Would it be effective to change instruments for different sections?
- Plan your performance, and look for ways of improving it.
- A careful use of percussion can help.

By planning in this way, you will soon have your own folk band.

Compose a **D1** melody in similar style, using the doh hexachord.

Invent a new structure to include your **D1** and **D2** melodies.

Perhaps some members of the class could invent
a dance and perform it with your folk band.

MUSIC
IN
OUR
LIVES

A three-part canon

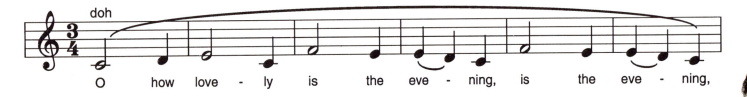

doh

O how love - ly is the eve - ning, is the eve - ning,

*

When the bells are sweet - ly ring - ing, sweet - ly ring - ing,

*

Ding, dong, ding, dong, ding, dong.

This is a traditional English melody.

Sing it as a group of three, and learn it by heart.

Now sing the melody as a three-part canon.

Play it from memory on a keyboard or pitched percussion instrument (doh = C).

Now play the melody as a three-part canon.

Then from memory, play the melody with doh = G.

Check this analysis:

1 structure A B C
2 6-bar phrases
3 ¾ time signature
4 doh hexachord on C
5 repetition
6 sequence

Fiddle-de-dee

Work with a partner. Sing, then play, these two pieces.

Tell me, shep-her-dess, where have you been? To a hum-ble sta-ble

where a babe was born, Born of Mo-ther Ma - ry on this hap-py morn.

Fid-dle-de-dee, Fid-dle-de-dee, the fly has mar-ried the bum-ble bee, Says the fly, says he, "Will you mar-ry me, and

live with me,— sweet bum-ble bee?" Fid-dle-de-dee, Fid-dle-de-dee, the fly has mar-ried the bum-ble bee.

Composing by yourself (1)

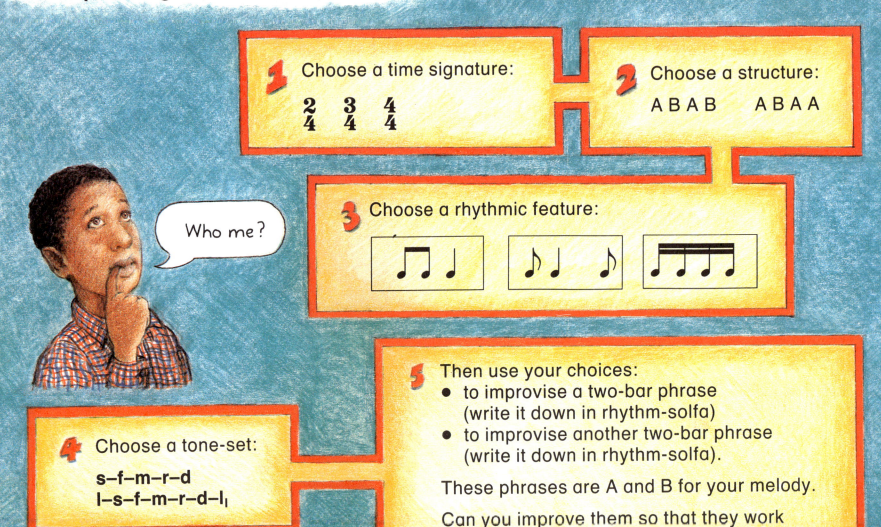

1 Choose a time signature:

$\frac{2}{4}$ $\frac{3}{4}$ $\frac{4}{4}$

2 Choose a structure:

A B A B   A B A A

Who me?

3 Choose a rhythmic feature:

5 Then use your choices:
- to improvise a two-bar phrase (write it down in rhythm-solfa)
- to improvise another two-bar phrase (write it down in rhythm-solfa).

These phrases are A and B for your melody.

Can you improve them so that they work well together within a structural pattern?

Perform your phrases to a partner.

4 Choose a tone-set:

s–f–m–r–d
l–s–f–m–r–d–lₗ

Composing by yourself (2)

6 Using the structure you chose, write out the complete melody in staff notation.

7 Ask someone to sing or play your piece.
What does s/he think?

8 Is it best performed by voice or instruments?

If voice, why not write some words?

Choose a topic:
Easter   A seaside visit   My favourite pet

9 How could you extend this melody to make it:
– 16 bars long?
– or 24 bars long?

. . . Why not?

Can you think of improvements?

Fanfares

Fanfares are usually played on brass instruments.
Bugles and simple trumpets play only on certain notes –
basically, doh–me–soh.

As pieces of music, fanfares are often quite short.

Here are two fanfares. Play them on an instrument.

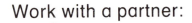

So, by using only d-m-s it is easy to compose fanfares.

Work with a partner:

1 Think when fanfares might be used.

2 Compose a fanfare in ⁴⁄₄ . Write two, three, or four bars only
  in staff notation. Include sixteenth notes because these
  sound impressive on brass instruments.

An important new pentachord

Pentachords do not need to start only on doh.

Pentachords can be based on other notes.

One of the most useful pentachords starts on the note lah.

The doh pentachord

d   r   m   f   s

COMPARE

The lah pentachord

l,   t   d   r   m

Work with a partner in the following ways:

- Together, sing the doh pentachord, then the lah pentachord.
- Then one partner hums either the doh or lah pentachord (ascending or descending); the other repeats, singing to solfa.
- Then one partner sings, to solfa, either the doh or lah pentachord (ascending or descending); the other follows by singing, to solfa, the other pentachord.

This melody uses the lah pentachord.

One lit-tle can-dle burn, burn, burn, Ha-nuk-kah is here.

One lit-tle can-dle bright and clear, Ha-nuk-kah is here.

- Sing the melody to solfa.
- Sing the song to the words.
- Sing the song in canon with a partner.
- Play the melody from memory on an instrument, with lah = D.

The pentachord on l, (a new note – te)   p.63   **39**

Making a climax

Use percussion instruments to produce a climax for:

- winning a race
- having a nice surprise
- being frightened in the dark.

Did you try:

A STARTING SLOWLY, GETTING FASTER?
B STARTING QUIETLY, GETTING LOUDER?
C STARTING SIMPLY, GETTING MORE COMPLEX?

With a partner, can you think of any more climax situations and make suitable music for one of them?

Consider using voices as well as instruments.

Writing in staff notation (doh = C), compose a melody using these ideas:

- 8 or 16 bars
- lah pentachord or doh hexachord + l₁
- $\frac{3}{4}$ or $\frac{4}{4}$
- sequence/repetition
- structure

Then perform your melody to make a climax.
Experiment with the methods A, B and C.

Hand-me-down melodies

Folk songs are songs which are passed from one generation
to another. Often, they tell a story about a special event.
These songs were not usually written down.
Singers sometimes altered the words and melody,
or added new words to songs they had heard.

Choose a song you know well. Alter the words and melody.
Perform the new version.

me

Oh Ma - dam I will give to you the keys of Can - ter - bu - ry,_____ And

all the bells of Lon - don shall ring to make us mer - ry,_____ If

you will be my joy,_____ my sweet and on - ly dear,_____ And

come a - long with me a - ny - where.

This song uses
the lah
pentachord on D.
Sing it to solfa,
then to the words.

Lullabies

Lullabies, like folk songs, have been handed down from one generation to another.

Can you remember a lullaby which was sung to you when you were a baby?

Here Is a lullaby from Sweden.

Sing it and memorise it.

With a partner, work out the most suitable way of performing this piece.

Decide your tempo, dynamics (loudness), starting pitch and how you will use your voice.

Compose a lullaby

1 Compose a lullaby in $\frac{2}{4}$ or $\frac{6}{8}$, using the lah pentachord.

2 Write your rhythm first, based on these words:

Sleep, my dearest baby,
Sleep, my dearest son.
Silent is the evening
Now the day is done.

3 Improvise your melody and write it in rhythm-solfa (Writing Sheet 2).

4 Then transcribe your melody into staff notation – lah pentachord on D (Writing Sheet 2).

lah

Hush - a - bye, my   lit - tle   babe,   Now   it's   time   for
Hush - a - bye, my   lit - tle   babe,   Ti - ny   stars   are

sleep - ing.   See the dark-ness   all   a - round.   All God's crea-tures
peep - ing.

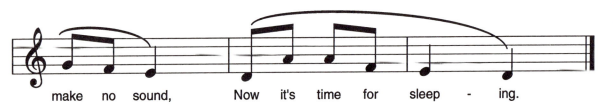

make   no   sound,   Now   it's   time   for   sleep - ing.

Passing notes

Here is a simple melody, without passing notes.

Jo likes to include as many passing notes as possible in his composing. So, Jo has rewritten the melody like this:

Louise thinks a melody can be spoiled by having too many passing notes. So, Louise has rewritten the melody like this:

Sing or play the melodies written by Jo and Louise.
What are the differences?
Perform the melodies several times, changing the tempo and dynamics each time. Does it make any difference to your opinion?

Working with a partner, rewrite this new melody on Writing Sheet 1, adding passing notes where you think they are suitable.

Compare your melody with versions written and performed by other pairs.

Using delayed and passing notes

Here are six melodic ideas.

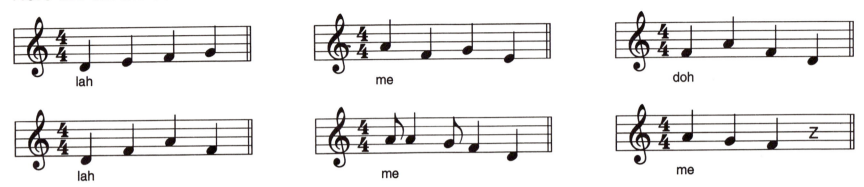

Rewrite them to include delayed notes and passing notes (Writing Sheet 1).

Devise several 4-bar melodies by combining your revised versions of these bars.

The melodies will need structure (e.g. A B C A) – so some bars might be used more than once.

Form a group of four and, without writing them down,
take turns to sing or play your 4-bar melodies to each other.

Make a recording of the best melodies.

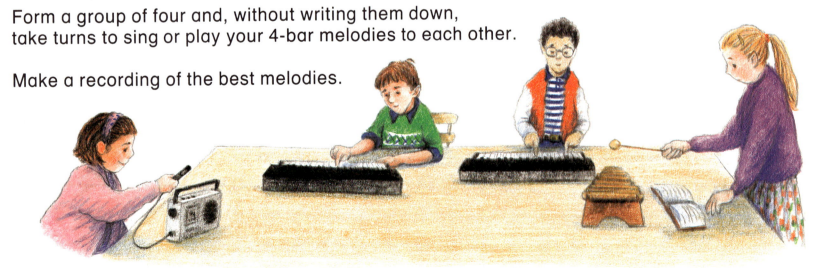

Composing with delayed and passing notes

Work with a partner.

Rewrite the following (to include delayed notes and passing notes) and add them to the collection on your Writing Sheet 1 from page 44.

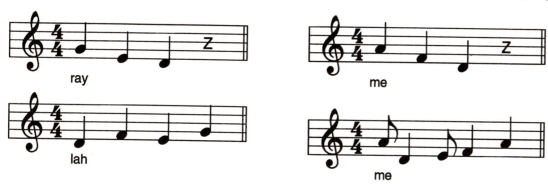

ray

me

lah

me

Choose five bars from the 10 examples on your Writing Sheet 1 and call them **a, b, c, d, e.**

Now construct a 12-bar melody, using this structure – or something similar:

A (4 bars)	B (4 bars)	A (4 bars)
a b a c	d e d e	a b a c

Write your melody in staff notation on your Writing Sheet.

Sing and play your finished melody to others in the class.

A supporters' song

Perhaps you play sports at your school.

Some sports are played in teams, with spectators cheering and singing songs.

Here are the words of a 'supporters' song'.

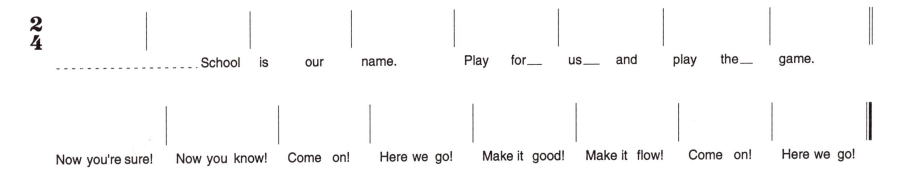

School is our name. Play for us and play the game.

Now you're sure! Now you know! Come on! Here we go! Make it good! Make it flow! Come on! Here we go!

Some words have a line after them, like this _____. This means that these syllables have more than one note in the melody.

Ask your teacher for Copymaster Worksheet 3. Work with a partner and compose a melody for this 'supporters' song', using the words shown.

Working with melody

Sing this melody with your partner.
Learn to sing it from memory.

m   l̦ ț d r m   m   r d ț r d ț l̦ m   l̦ ț d r m   r   d ț l̦

Now, perform it with one partner singing the melody as the other partner taps this ostinato rhythm:

Can you sing the melody and tap the rhythm at the same time?

Write the melody in staff notation (lah = A).

Play it on a keyboard, as your partner taps the ostinato on a percussion instrument.

Here is another melody.
Sing it with your partner.
Learn to sing it from memory.

l̦ m m m   ț d r d ț d ț l̦   l̦ m m m   ț d r d ț l̦

Perform an extended version of this melody by singing it twice, but as follows:

8 bars – lah pentachord	4 bars – doh pentachord	4 bars – lah pentachord

A building song

When her cottage in the village burned down, the old woman who lived there had nowhere to go. So the other villagers decided to build a new one for her.

Sing this 'Building song' with a partner. Then play it on a keyboard.

(Villager 1)
me I will build, build the walls to be strong and thick. I will build, build the roof out of (Villager 2)

(Villager 3)
thatch and stick, I have win-dows to make which are tall and wide, And then (Villager 4)

(All) (Chorus)
I'll de-co-rate so it's snug in-side. We will build, build, build 'til the

work is done, We will build, build, build 'til the set of sun.

Compose a melody for these new words. Use $\frac{3}{4}$ time and an A B A C structure. Complete an Analysis Sheet first.

We have built you a cottage in the village,
Near your friends and your neighbours again.
With your animals you can live contented,
Warm and sheltered from wind and from rain.

MUSIC
IN
OUR
LIVES